Most plants in a garden grow from seeds.

1

The gardener sows his seeds.

The peas in a pea pod
are seeds.

The beans in a bean pod
are seeds.

Have you sown seeds in your garden?
You can grow some seeds in your classroom.

Put some blotting paper on a saucer.
Pour some water on the blotting paper.
Put some cress seeds on the blotting paper.

Place the saucer on a sunny
window sill.

Keep the blotting paper
damp.

Soon you will see the cress
seeds growing.

Grow a bean plant.

Put a roll of blotting paper in a jam jar.

Place a bean seed inside the jar so that you can see it.

Put some sand in the jar.

Pour a cup of water over it.

Place the jam jar on a window sill.

Keep the sand in the jam jar damp.

Draw a picture of your bean plant every four days.

Grow an oak plant.

Find an acorn under an oak tree.

Plant the acorn in some damp
earth in a plant pot.

Watch it grow.

Make a list of the seeds you can find in the woods and
fields.

Say where you find them.

Grow an apple plant and an orange plant.

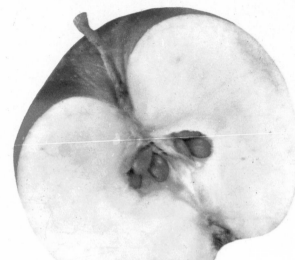

The pip in an apple
is a seed.

The pip in an orange is
a seed.

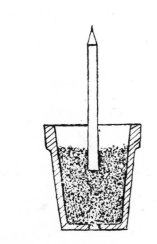

Fill two plant pots with soil.

Make a hole in each with a pencil.

Put a brown apple pip in one hole and an orange pip in the other.

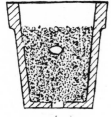

Cover them with soil.

Keep the soil damp.

Place them on a sunny window sill.

Soon you will see some green shoots growing.

They will grow into a small apple tree and a small orange tree.

Seeds need sunshine to make them grow.

Sunshine gives warmth and light.

Seeds need water to make them grow.

Try this experiment.

In three jam jars put
    a roll of blotting paper,
    some dry sand,
    and a bean.

Pour some water in one jam
jar and place on a sunny
window sill.

Leave the sand in the second
jam jar dry and place on
a sunny window sill.

Pour some water in the last
jam jar and put in a cold place
such as a refrigerator.

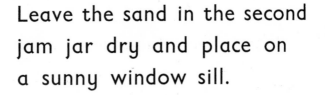

Do all the seeds grow?

Try this experiment.

Put a plant growing in a pot in a dark cupboard.

After a few days take it out.

The leaves will be white because they need light.

Try this experiment.

Put a piece of wood on some green grass.

After a few days take it off.

The grass will be white because the grass needs light.

Seeds find new homes in different ways.

Some seeds are planted by the gardener in the garden.

Some seeds, like the acorn from the oak tree, fall on the ground and grow there.

Other seeds are carried to new homes by the wind.

Sycamore seeds have propellers to help them sail along.

Dandelion seeds have parachutes to help them sail along.

Make a list of all the seeds which are carried by the wind.

Other seeds are carried by animals to new homes.

Goose grass has prickly seeds which stick to the fur of animals.

The squirrel hides nuts for winter.

Sometimes he forgets them and these nuts grow into new trees.

Other seeds are carried by birds in their beaks.

Some seeds are carried by ducks in their webbed feet.

Make a list of seeds which are carried by birds and animals.

Other seeds are carried by water.

Some plants are not grown from seeds.

Some plants grow from bulbs.

An onion grows from a bulb.

A daffodil grows from a bulb.

In the Autumn plant a hyacinth bulb in a jar of water so that the bulb is sitting on the water.

Soon whole roots will grow
from the bottom of the bulb.

Then a green shoot will grow
from the top of the bulb.

Then the flower will grow.

Make a list of plants which
will grow from bulbs.

Some plants grow from corms.

A crocus grows from a corm.

See if you can find the difference between a corm and a bulb.

Some plants grow from tubers.

Potatoes are tubers.

When we eat potatoes we are eating tubers.

The gardener plants potato tubers to grow new potatoes.

Some plants grow from cuttings.

Cut a stem from a currant
bush. Cut it just below a bud.

Plant it in the garden.

It will grow into a new
currant bush.

Try this with a geranium.

Cut a stem from a geranium.

Leave two or three leaves at one end.

Plant it in a pot.

It will grow into a new geranium.

We have learnt :

Many plants grow from seeds.

Some plants grow from bulbs,
                                    corms,
                                    tubers,
                                    cuttings.

To grow properly, plants must have warmth,
                                              water,
                                              and light.

Acknowledgement

We wish to thank:

JOHN ARMITAGE F.R.P.S. for supplying the photograph
on page 14.

Printed and Published in Great Britain by E. J. ARNOLD & SON LIMITED LEEDS   © 1966

AP/0200/02/P3965